HERITAGE CLASSICS

Dr. Pawan Pokhariyal
pdrpawan@rediffmail.com

TENANTS

(A Play within a Play)

AND

THE SEMINAR

(A Play on importance and purpose of Science)

HERITAGE

HERITAGE PUBLISHERS
NEW DELHI

HERITAGE PUBLISHERS
19-A, Ansari Road, Daryaganj,
New Delhi - 110 002
Tel .: 23266258, 23264444
Fax.: 23263050
E-mail : heritage@nda.vsnl.net.in

ISBN : 9788170262664

Printed in India
Sagar Printers, 23 Ansari Road,
New Delhi - 110 002

Author's Note

The play "Seminar" discusses the importance of science in the form of a play. The play presents only the basic aspects pertaining to science. The process of learning has been used as a means to discuss the role of science because learning is common to each one of us. The play also presents the role of Nature in guiding us to seek the exactness and truth of life. The play "Tenants" which has been already published previously is being published once again to keep the relevance of Art and Science together. The play "Tenants" contains the philosophy of art and "Seminar" presents the philosophy of science. The story in both the plays is connected in order to show the relevance of both art and science together. For the same reason both the plays can be staged together.

Professor Prakrati says in "Seminar", " Art has the ability to give satisfaction and happiness with ones own work and science has the capability to inculcate in us the aptitude to search for the truth".

Both the plays are also about the relevance of art

and science in the scheme of life.

In the play “Tenants” Professor Soul presents an artful perspective of life and tells Professor Mind “Dear Mind we must remain grateful to life for allowing us to be together and witness a wonderful play of life unfold itself”.

In the play “Seminar” Professor Self presents a similar and scientific perspective of life and says “We must be grateful to life for giving us an opportunity to be together and learn so much and associate with each other as scientist in our endeavour to decipher science and learn through a wonderful seminar about science, arts and life.

Professor Prakrati adds further and says

“Professor Self let me add a little more. We must be grateful to life for giving us an opportunity to be together, to associate and relate with Nature and search for exactness and truth of life. And let me repeat the seminar is just an example, the extension is to the entire life”.

The characters chosen in the plays have a philosophical, artistical and scientific relevance. Their names are indicative of the role each character is playing in the play.

TENANTS

(A play within a play)

Characters

PROFESSOR SOUL/ SELF: A scientist at the university.

PROFESSOR MIND: Professor of philosophy.

CAPTAIN BRAIN: Newly appointed bank manager of university bank.

MISS / LADY HEART: Teacher in the primary school for the children of the university staff.

Scene of Action

An impressive looking newly constructed double storey bungalow in the midst of a clean and peaceful locality. A beautiful garden all around the house.

A straight pathway through the garden takes us to the verandah of the house covered by a portico supported upon round pillars. An entrance door ahead of the verandah opens into the reception hall, well furnished and sparkling clean. In the center of the reception hall are sofas arranged around the central round table. A door on the right opens into anteroom and an adjoining bedroom and a door on the left opens into the study and an adjoining office room.

A back door opens into the dining hall and an adjoining kitchen. A staircase from the left side of the house takes us to the upper floor where Professor Soul resides. The construction and arrangement is same as the ground floor.

Act I

Captain Brain and Miss Heart who are young recently engaged couple have came to meet Professor Soul to take the ground floor of house on rent. Professor Soul has a calm face radiating intelligence and a seriousness of purpose. Eyes are filled with a childish inquisitiveness as if trying to learn.

Captain Brain is young smart and intelligent looking and has been recently appointed as a bank manager of the university bank . Miss Heart is a teacher in a primary school within the university campus. She is young, pretty and charming woman and her countenance display youthful excitement.

Every one is seated in the reception hall. Professor Soul in the center sofa. Captain Brain on the left side and Miss Heart on the right side. There are few cups on the table and a plate full of snacks.

MISS HEART: We have finally found a place of our liking Professor. Isn't it Brain?

CAPT. BRAIN: Yes dear.

MISS HEART: I like the garden and the locality as well. The neighbourhood seems to be decent and peace loving.

CAPT. BRAIN: Are all of them working at the University Professor?

PROF. SOUL: Yes most of them. The area is close to the university and is mostly inhabited by the university staff who have given up their official residences and have settled here itself. Just few years back there was a straight road, which connected the university and the city. Today an entire township has sprouted along it.

CAPT. BRAIN: The house seems to be newly constructed, Professor.

PROF. SOUL: Yes, I decided to reconstruct the house to keep it in sync with the times.

CAPT. BRAIN: We are happy Professor that you responded so quickly to the ad that we gave in the newspaper. It would have been an ordeal to drive everyday to the university from our city residence and again back home during evening. Let me tell you in detail.

I have been appointed as a new bank manager at the university bank and Miss Heart too has been working as a teacher in the primary school for the children of the university staff. My bank has provided me with a residence inside the city and as I told you before that daily driving shall be very cumbersome. Miss Heart's school has given her a room in the women's hostel which won't be useful as we have got recently engaged and shall require a bigger accommodation for both of us. So finally we decided to rent a house till further arrangements are made.

PROF. SOUL: It does seem strange to me that the bank doesn't provide official residence nearby. However you need not thank me. After the reconstruction, I was also looking for someone who would look after the house properly. The university work keeps me pretty busy. Every month there is some seminar or presentation in other universities which keeps me busy for days together.

MISS HEART: Don't worry Professor, I am of the kind, who likes cleanliness and purity around and Brain is also a disciplined man. As long as we stay here we will maintain the house in proper shape and condition.

PROF. SOUL: I am delighted to hear that Miss Heart.

CAPT. BRAIN: Professor, regarding the rent shall it remain the same as was mentioned in the letter or are there any extra charges?

MISS HEART: We can ask about these details after shifting here Brain.

PROF. SOUL: Miss Heart, Captain Brain is the bank manager and he has learnt well to verify the necessary accounts and transaction properly and it is appropriate to clarify so that our companionship remain durable enough to last long.The rent shall remain the same.

CAPT. BRAIN: Indeed Professor we too would like our companionship to last long , and to finalise we would meet you tomorrow and complete all official formalities. We shall be shifting here soon.

PROF. SOUL: Fine captain. The captain in your name still surprises me.

CAPT. BRAIN: Professor, It so happened that after completing my studies in mathematics and economics, I joined the defence services to keep with our family tradition for a few years. Later I decided to continue with my interest and passed the banking exams. I joined the training institute of the bank but continued to be called captain by my family members.

PROF. SOUL: Are all the male members in your family still employed in defence ?

CAPT. BRAIN: It was so earlier Professor. At my grandfather's time and even previously, almost all the male members of the clan were employed in defence. It was source of honour and livelihood. Gradually the trends have changed. It started with the distant uncle of mine who settled for farming. Today their generation is the owner of large farms, producing all sorts of agricultural products. In our present generation few of my cousins have become computer engineers, others are in business. Few of my cousins continue to be in defence. If we study the entire family chart today the family members have ventured in all sorts of professions.

PROF. SOUL: Interesting Captain. And how about your family Miss Heart? Women these days are sure coming up fast. There are few women Professors in our university who are doing quite well.

MISS HEART: Correct Professor. The females in our family too have entered into all sorts of professions. Just few generations back most of them were respectable wives and homemakers. Then few took up profession like beauticians and office assistants. I decided to become a teacher at the primary school. A distant niece of mine is an interior decorator, another is a doctor. So over all our family too is getting diversified into all sorts of professions, earning their own livelihood.

CAPT. BRAIN: Tell us something about your family Professor. Is everyone a scientist?

PROF. SOUL: As far as I have been told and remember everyone has been a scientist. Some succeeded at the highest level at their times. Some didn't make it big. I am happy that everyone made some contribution to science. More than inventions and discoveries that everyone thought of life in one way or the other and also about means of improvement, makes me glad and the quest continues and shall continue.

MISS HEART: Till when Professor?

PROF. SOUL: Till perfection Miss Heart. Till

perfection.

(A thoughtful silence ensues for a while.)

CAPT. BRAIN: The journey ahead seems inspiring Professor. We eagerly look forward to staying with you.

PROF. SOUL: Sure Captain. I too shall eagerly await your arrival.

CAPT. BRAIN: Every thing finalized between us Professor. We meet again tomorrow for completing the formalities.

PROF. SOUL: I'll keep the papers ready Captain.

(Captain Brain and Miss. Heart get up to leave.)

CAPT. BRAIN / Miss. HEART: Good bye Professor.

PROF. SOUL: Good bye Captain. Good bye Miss Heart.

(Miss Heart and Capt. Brain leave the reception hall.)

ACT II

As per the tradition of Miss. Heart's family her name has become Lady Heart after the marriage.

Captain Brain and Lady Heart have already shifted to the house. It's almost a month and all of them have become close enough and often share morning breakfast together.

It's Sunday again and after finishing their breakfast, Professor Soul and Captain Brain are seated together in a garden chair around a round plastic table under the shade in the garden. Lady Heart is tending to few flowers nearby.

PROF. SOUL: You both seem to be well settled here and I must admire the improved interior decoration of the house carried out by both of you.

CAPT. BRAIN: Indeed we have got well adjusted to the house and the surroundings Professor. We have made few changes inside and the credit for it goes to Heart for having taken keen interest in decorating the house. I just got her whatever she needed for doing so.

PROF. SOUL: *(Addressing Lady Heart who is still busy with the flowers)* You seem to have special interest in gardening as well, Lady Heart.

LADY HEART: *(Nostalgically)* It is influence of my childhood Professor. I have spent much of my childhood away from hustle bustle of city life in proximity to nature. The free and open fields, the fresh air, the beautiful landscapes and the natural gardens have left a long lasting impression upon me. Oh! how I wish nature was allowed to remain in all her pristine and poetic beauty.

CAPT. BRAIN: I am happy Professor that the university, the locality and the house are compatible with the likings of both of us. Whenever I take Heart to the city, she keeps questioning and doesn't seem to be comfortable among the concrete structures we have erected. Actually Professor I am a complete city bred kind. The primary influence upon me has been of the castles, bridges, buildings and all other technological advancements that we have achieved. Here at the university there is plenty of greenery and gardens to keep Heart happy and I like the architecture of the buildings, which is quite exquisite and town planning excellent.

PROF. SOUL: Indeed I too find the university and the surrounding town a balanced blend of both the natural and the modern. Let me tell you about myself also, I have lived in all sorts of circumstances and environments. My grandfather was a botanist and had his house and lab near the countryside full of herbs and shrubs. I spent my childhood among those herbs and shrubs with my grandfather. I shifted to a small town where my parents were part of a research team studying genetics and evolution. My education then took me to a city where I worked as a student of modern physics. My own interest later brought me to the present university where I continued the family tradition of research. And in spite of so many years in research, I find life more mysterious than ever before.

(A thoughtful silence ensues for a while.)

LADY HEART: Professor just like the interior decoration, I would like to make few amends in the garden as well.

PROF. SOUL: Sure Lady Heart, I told you the other day as well that my work keeps me busy. It's good that the house and the garden have found both of you as caretakers. I can safely use all my time in research work.

LADY HEART: Thanks Professor.

PROF. SOUL: Have both of you visited all the tourist spots nearby?

CAPT. BRAIN: Almost Professor. Heart has shown me all the tourist spots nearby.

PROF. SOUL: Do tell me when both of you are free

on a Sunday evening.

CAPT. BRAIN: Professor we are lucky to be free today itself. Tell us if you have anything interesting to suggest.

PROF. SOUL: The university has an art centre with a famous theatre and an art gallery within the campus. The university regularly holds art exhibitions in the gallery and also screens a play regularly by the university theatre group, comprising of young talented actors and actresses. The programmes are held every Sunday. Whenever you feel like accompanying me you can take free passes.

LADY HEART: Do they hold any traditional art exhibitions as well?

PROF. SOUL: Yes. Traditional art exhibition are held quite often in the gallery. I shall provide you with a monthly calendar of the programmes so that you could decide accordingly.

CAPT. BRAIN: I am also interested in paintings Professor.

PROF. SOUL: Then I must say that I have found wonderful companions with whom the journey to the art centre would become more interesting.

CAPT. BRAIN: And it may happen the journey to the art centre might awaken the little artist in us.

PROF. SOUL: Indeed Captain. There is no limitation to awaken the little artist in us. Take these passes along with today's programme. Both of you can decide and tell me before evening, an hour before the scheduled timings. We shall walk together to the centre.

(Professor Soul gives the passes and the programme list to the Lady Heart who studies them intently.)

PROF. SOUL: Well it has been a pleasant morning. First the breakfast and then the interesting talk we have had.

LADY HEART: It's already getting sunny. We must shift indoors.

CAPT. BRAIN: Yes, we should finish our daily chores for the day and few other official files, to keep ourselves free to go with Professor Soul.

(They all get up from their seats and walk towards the pathway. Their faint voices could still be heard.)

LADY HEART: The garden seems to be preparing for the spring Professor.
The flowers are ready to bloom......

PROF. SOUL: Still early Lady Heart. Yes the condition is healthy and a careful nurturing shall surely herald a happy spring.

(And their voices gradually become whispers.)

Act - III

It's almost a year since Captain Brain and Lady Heart have stayed with Professor Soul and all of them have shared a cordial relationship together. The house itself has remained in good condition as before and the garden has become more beautiful.

Captain Brain and Lady Heart have become regular visitors of the art gallery. It's a Sunday evening again. Lady Heart is in the kitchen and Captain is in his study when the door bell rings. Captain Brain opens the door .

CAPT. BRAIN: Welcome Professor. It's been almost a month you visited us. Heart Told me that you were out of town for a seminar.

PROF. SOUL: Yes Captain. The seminar was organized on a very short notice. The topics were of critical importance and the discussion turned out to be very fruitful.

(Lady Heart enters the hall with a plate of snacks and a tray with glasses containing fruit juice. She offers both of them a glass each and puts the plate

on the table. Professor Soul notices the new paintings and decorative vases in the house.)

PROF. SOUL: Plenty seems to have changed here since my last visit. New paintings, decorative vases and other works of traditional art.

CAPT. BRAIN: It's all your inspiration Professor. We have become regular visitors of the art gallery and have purchased all these paintings and other items very recently while you were attending the seminar. And you still haven't seen all the traditional art works that Heart has stocked up in other rooms. We have spent most of the interest of our savings on the purchase of the art work.

PROF. SOUL: I must compliment both of you for the interest you have shown towards the works of art. It's always useful to spend some of our income on works of art.

LADY HEART: We have surpassed our own imagination Professor. Everyone has praised our collection and many of my relatives have sought our advice on selecting art works.

CAPT. BRAIN: It has been a learning process for us Professor. I have bought many books on paintings, painters and different styles. Before you came, I was reading such a book in the study.

PROF. SOUL: Interesting Captain. And the little artist, has there been an awakening?

CAPT. BRAIN: Yes, Professor. Our interest in

art has brought both of us much closer. Heart turned out to be a poetess. She has written many poems on nature and love. She never told me before. She even sang a few of them the other day. Even I used to write during my college days. I let her read few of my essays on the achievements and evolution of civilization.

PROF. SOUL: The more we evolve the more revealing life becomes. Both of you could have prepared something together.

CAPT. BRAIN: For the first time after coming to the house we have felt like coming up with something more sublime and purer together. Let me be a little frank with you Professor and tell you in detail. You have seen both of us a happy couple always made for each other. Consider now our opinions. Are there any similarities? She likes nature in her original pristine beauty and I like the modern achievements, the city and the modern architecture. She likes poetry and I prefer prose. She likes traditional art and I like modern paintings. And it seemed to me that there were barely any similarities between us. Sometimes I wondered as to how long can the relationship be sustained.

LADY HEART: In fact it would have never happened. He was then busy with his career and on the other hand was me, who regarded love as essential and important. We met at the party for the first time and initially there was romance. Later we started debating on every aspect of life. Our families tried to convince us that we both could compliment each other and also that it was inevitable for us to be together to continue the race and so the tradition must be followed. We agreed with the advice and for a long while complimented each other well, preventing extremes of us. We then began to search for the elusive common, something sublime and pure to sustain our relationship.

CAPT. BRAIN: And then we started visiting the art gallery and specifically your words about awakening the little artist worked wonders and helped us discover the part of us which was sublime and pure – the artist. It took us a while Professor however the very discovery that life could be more profound than we ever thought filled us with inspiration and jubilation. We have decided to come up with something which would express the jubilation of discovering ourselves.

PROF. SOUL: Let us look at it positively. Even though both of you are of separate natures, I can make out that both of you are ready to accept the balance. You have already arrived at the sublime consensus, which shall be rewarding for both of you.

LADY HEART: You continue to inspire us Professor.

PROF. SOUL: Whenever I require inspiration , I begin to think of life and every inspiration begins to arrive naturally. It is important to let ourselves be calm and in tranquility the very life begins to express through us creatively.

(A thoughtful silence ensues for a while.)

PROF. SOUL: Well if both of you are looking for some help, then I have something good to tell you both. Professor Mind who is newly appointed Professor of philosophy in the university shall be coming to stay with us for few days. Coincidentally Professor Mind and our family have long term ties and many members have closely worked together on many research projects. When I read the new appointment on the university notice board I called up Professor Mind and asked him to stay with us for few days. Interestingly Professor Mind is also a playwright and has staged many plays previously. If everything goes fine, we will work out something during his stay to keep the little artist flourishing.

CAPT. BRAIN: Have arrangements been made for his stay Professor?

PROF. SOUL: Yes Captain. I have arranged for him a room next to the study. He is a voracious reader. He'll like to be close to the study. We met long back before the reconstruction of the house at the seminar, when he presented his paper on perception. It'll be interesting to meet him again.

LADY HEART: We too shall be vey happy to welcome Professor Mind to the house.

CAPT. BRAIN: Tell us Professor if we could be of any help.

PROF. SOUL: Sure Captain. Professor Mind has certain concepts of his own. Always works with them. You too shall find him interesting when you meet him.

CAPT. BRAIN: Already sounds interesting Professor.

PROF. SOUL: We shall meet again, when Professor Mind is here with us. Good bye till then.

(Professor Soul gets up.)

CAPT. BRAIN / LADY HEART: Good bye Professor.

(Professor Soul leaves the hall.)

ACT IV

Reception hall of the upper floor. The design and the arrangement is same as the ground floor except for the simplicity of the decoration. Professor Mind has already shifted to the house. He is an athletic looking Professor.
Professor Soul and Professor Mind are sitting on the centre sofa and having a talk. When the door bells rings, Captain Brain and Lady Heart enter inside.

PROF. SOUL: Captain Brain and Lady Heart, meet Professor Mind the newly appointed Professor of philosophy at the university. And Professor Mind, meet Captain Brain and Lady Heart. Captain Brain is the manager of the university Bank and Lady Heart is teacher at the university school.

(They all exchange greetings.Lady Heart and Captain Brain take their seats on adjacent sofas.)

PROF. MIND: Professor Soul was just telling me about both of you and about how close you have become to him in just a short span of time.

LADY HEART: Professor Soul has treated us as his own family members and along with him, we have discovered a lot about ourselves.

PROF. SOUL: We must be grateful to life for giving us an opportunity to be together in first place. Professor Mind has joined us and let us try to utilize his abilities in further enrichment and development.

PROF. MIND: Tell me Professor how could I best serve the enrichment process you just spoke of?

PROF. SOUL: In many ways Professor Mind. I was telling you about how Captain Brain and Lady Heart got interested in art works which helped in discovering the writer and the poetess in them. I told them about your abilities as a playwright and since then their wish to prepare something which could be presented on stage has acquired new wings.

PROF. MIND: Professor Soul is always full of inspiration and keeps motivating everyone. I would suggest you both to first have a look at my work. I have planned to arrange a short play to be enacted by the theatre group of the university. After and when both of you agree, I shall compose a play with both of you in major roles. Will that suit both of you? The entire preparation shall take a month or so. And yes, Professor Soul told me about the writer and the poetess in you. I promise we all shall work in close collaboration and come up with something wonderful.

CAPT. BRAIN: We are ecstatic and exalted by

the interest both of you have shown towards us. It'll require lot of preparation Professor.

LADY HEART: And encouragement as well. Its not very often that we have performed on stage.

PROF. SOUL: I'll call it modesty Lady Heart. There are many roles both of you have played together. On stage shall be much easier as the script shall be ready and there shall be many practice sessions before.

CAPT. BRAIN: We shall put all our efforts and ensure our full co-operation, Professor Mind. Professor Soul told us that Professor Mind shall be staying with us only till his official residence is ready. Will it effect our plans in any way?

LADY HEART: How good it would be if Professor Mind could stay here with us.

PROF. SOUL: I like the suggestion. And if Professor Mind agrees I shall be equally happy. We have planned a few research projects together. It would become much easier.

PROF. MIND: Professor, please don't take any extra troubles for me. I shall be provided with an official residence soon.

PROF. SOUL: It won't be troublesome to me in anyway Professor Mind. In fact it would be good for the research projects we have planned together. I have been passing through the most critical phase of my work and have planned a small lab on the top floor of the house so that I could put some extra efforts into my research. I shall be staying in my lab after that and the entire middle floor shall be for Professor Mind.

LADY HEART: It sounds wonderful Professor. You have already planned it properly. We can expect a positive response from Professor Mind.

PROF. MIND: I am overwhelmed and happy for the warm invitation. I too am a scientist like Professor Soul and the only aspect of importance to me is that my residence should be close to my work. Apart from the research work that Professor Soul has planned, the progress of my own projects depends on Professor Soul's research. It will be necessary for me to cooperate.

(Everyone smiles.)

PROF. SOUL: Your decision has brought immense joy to all of us Professor. We look forward to promising days ahead.

CAPT. BRAIN: Indeed Professor. We both can expect to learn a lot from Professor Mind.

PROF. SOUL: To start with, here are passes for the short play, which Professor Mind is organizing on his arrival. The play is on a philosophical theme.

(Gives two passes to Captain Brain and Lady Heart.)

PROF. SOUL: The play shall be staged on coming Saturday followed by a small function as a welcome to Professor Mind.

CAPT. BRAIN: Both of us shall surely be present

for the programme Professor. Come Heart we must allow the old comrades to plan their future activities with each other.

LADY HEART: Oh yes.

(Both get up to leave.)

PROF. MIND: It was pleasant talking to both of you. Keep visiting. Soon we will have to prepare and work together on the play.

CAPT. BRAIN: Sure Professor.

(They bid goodbye and leave the hall.)

Act –V

Captain Brain and Lady Heart have come to visit Professor Mind. Over the few days they have become very close. Professor Soul is busy with the reconstruction of the new floor of the house. It's a Sunday after the short play organized by Professor Mind on his arrival, was staged.

LADY HEART: The play presented yesterday was quite inspiring Professor. The performance of the actors and actresses was also commendable. Earlier we used to be regular visitors of the art gallery but in your company, we shall begin to like the theatre as well.

PROF. MIND: Thanks for the encouragement Lady Heart. Its good that you have started liking the theatre as well. It will help our future projects together. I have already started working on the play with both of you having major roles. Professor Soul has suggested me to prepare a naturalistic play with only a few technicalities to give it an overall purposeful look. We shall begin our practice sessions as soon as the play is ready. Tell me the days when both of you would be free for the practice.

CAPT. BRAIN: Saturday evenings and Sundays shall be most suitable to us Professor. We shall continue practicing on other days as well in our room. We shall try to put extra efforts if you want us to.

PROF. MIND: It shall be enough Captain. We'll just require a few weeks practice. There won't be much necessity of extra efforts.

All that is required will be to use your natural abilities and talents.

CAPT. BRAIN: Sure Professor.

LADY HEART: I too shall try my best Professor Mind.

CAPT. BRAIN: Where is Professor Soul? He too would have spoken few words of encouragement.

PROF. MIND: He is quite busy with the reconstruction of the new floor of the house. It's surprising that he has already started the lab work going in just a week. I wonder whether he had any influence in my appointment as Professor of Philosophy at the university. Anyhow its turning out to be worthwhile for me as my own research has acquired new momentum because of Professor Soul. He has this unique ability to inspire everyone around to get involved and interested in new activities, like the research projects which he has suggested.

Of late he keeps himself quite busy with his work.

LADY HEART: You are also much like him, Professor, always inspiring and encouraging. Both of you are similar in many ways. For instance both of you are always dedicated to your work. I wonder what made you remain a bachelor still?

PROF. MIND: Let me tell you both in detail. In childhood I was a bit erratic and regarded everything as a play. As youth approached it began to dawn upon me that I should be more serious and controlled. I began to organize myself and began to take my education seriously. I decided to be positive and gradually everything began to get resolved. I began to express myself in the form of theatrical plays and developed philosophical interests. Before I could get engaged anywhere I got engaged to my work and remained a bachelor still.

CAPT. BRAIN: Interesting. Professor Mind tell us about how Professor Soul and you got acquainted to each other? Were you both known to each other since childhood?

PROF. MIND: Professor Soul's family and ours were known to each other since many generations, for having worked together on many research projects and our parents tell us that we had been together even during our childhood. It must have been long back because I have only faint memories of being together. It was only during one of the science exhibitions at home town that I met him first, after I had grown into an adult. The exhibition held then has been inscribed still in my memories for many reasons. We had a seminar of sorts in which I presented a paper on perception. I asked him after the presentation that it must be more intricate as we dig deeper into the mysteries. He said, "Professor Mind, it does become more and more profound and yet more simple". We had just got acquainted to each other and within few hours we decided to co-operate on few research projects.

LADY HEART: So the decision to co-operate in the research projects was taken before you arrived at the house, Professor.

PROF. MIND: We had decided to co-operate long back. The rate at which we have progressed has surprised even me. And when I tell him, as to how wonderful it has been to work with him he repeats the same lines, "Professor Mind we should be grateful to life for having given us the opportunity of being together".

LADY HEART: It's the same case with us Professor. Professor Soul always treated us as his own family members. We have felt ourselves growing and evolving. We have become close to you as well and are getting a chance to express ourselves better. Tell us Professor

Mind, how to sustain the little artist in us?

PROF. MIND: I told you before that I tried utilizing the experiences of life to present as plays. I have been much influenced by what Professor Soul told me few days back, "Professor Mind art must come from within for which we should allow ourselves be calm. Once we are tranquil creativity begins to flow on her own. It will be like a child again, a little child busy with his play." As far as sustaining the artist is concerned, I have already told you that the play is getting ready.

CAPT. BRAIN: The play reminds me Professor about the hectic day you have had yesterday and we have already taken much of your time. We will take your permission for today.

(Captain Brain and Lady Heart get up to leave.)

PROF. MIND: Keep visiting Captain and Lady Heart. The longer we talk about our lives, the better and useful it will be for the play. Of course we will keep it as relevant and as precise as possible.

CAPT. BRAIN: Professor, have you decided the name of the play?

PROF. MIND: Yes Captain I have decided the name of the play. It shall be " Tenants - a play within the play".

LADY HEART: Thanks Professor we shall eagerly await the day when we start the practice sessions.

PROF. MIND: Sure, it shall be soon. It won't take

me more than a week to complete the play.

LADY HEART: Good. By next week we would be back from our visit to our parents house.

PROF. MIND: Are you visiting your parents house next week?

CAPT. BRAIN: True Professor.

PROF. MIND: Happy journey.

CAPT. BRAIN/LADY HEART: Thank you Professor. Good Bye.

(Captain Brain and Lady Heart bid good bye and leave the hall.)

Act –VI

Professor Mind's reception hall. Captain Brain and Lady Heart have come to meet Professor Mind soon after returning back from a visit to their parent's house.

LADY HEART: Have we heard it correct Professor that you and Professor Soul are going on some long journey?

PROF. MIND: Professor Soul and I are not going on some journey. We are going close to our hometown. He must have told you about it. Both of us have been promoted as HOD's of our departments and have been asked to report to the main branch of the university close to our hometown. It took him very long to arrive at a decision. He has decided in favour of the transfer as it would help us both in our scientific research and also help us know more about ourselves. The university has allowed us another week to convey our final decision.

CAPT. BRAIN: He used to tell us a lot about his

hometown. It's good that he is getting a chance to be close to his hometown. We haven't seen Professor Soul for last few days. In fact we were told about the transfer by our own colleagues.

PROF. MIND: Professor Soul is still in his room. He keeps himself very busy these days. Let me tell you both in detail. A few days back when I woke up at midnight, I discovered that Professor Soul wasn't asleep. It happened a few more nights. He used to walk ceaselessly in the reception hall above. I went to his floor at the midnight and saw him contemplating seriously in the reception hall. On ringing the bell he welcomed me and after a little talk about his research, he began to talk nostalgically about us. He also told me that we all make such a fine family. Lady Heart as a teacher of young students and maintaining the house so well. Captain Brain the Bank manager and the protector of the house. Me as Professor of Philosophy and as a playwright and himself as a scientist searching for solutions of the mysteries of life. He said the house should have a place where we could interact more frequently. Later he began to talk about his work again and the projects we finished together. Still later and only after questioning, he told me about our promotion and transfer. He told me about how he spent the entire day thinking about the decision he would make. He finally decided that we must shift to our hometown because better research facilities would help us arrive at results earlier.

CAPT. BRAIN: We must congratulate both of you on your promotion and also being transferred to the university main branch close to your hometown.

PROF. MIND: He told me, he would come on his own to meet both of you in the hall before he takes a final decision. He would soon be here.

LADY HEART: Professor Soul's hometown must be a nice place.

CAPT. BRAIN: Yes he told us about his hometown once. Here he comes.

(Professor Soul arrives in the reception hall.)

PROF. MIND: Welcome Professor, I told Captain and Lady Heart about our promotion and transfer. They were surprised and happy that we got promotion and by the fact that the transfer is close to our hometown.

PROF. SOUL: It was surprising to me as well. It has taken me a lot of time and yet I haven't arrived at a final decision. I wanted to talk to both of you before deciding on the transfer. As far as our research is concerned, I know I shall get better facilities near our hometown and will find it much easier to trace our lost cousin and niece.

LADY HEART: Lost cousin and niece! You never told us about them before.

PROF. MIND: It's a long story. I told you before that we met each other at a science exhibition for the first time. Well during the science exhibition I had brought my niece along and Professor Soul his cousin. Both were just few years old, barely able to walk on their own. During the exhibition we both were supposed to present our papers. We both had to go on stage simultaneously. We made both of them to sit with a colleague of ours. All of us became very busy during the presentation. Even our colleague, whom we had asked to look after our cousin and niece, never noticed , when both of them slipped and walked out of the hall. It was only after the presentation that we realized our cousin and niece were missing. We made hectic search for them after that, looked around every nook and corner of the exhibition. It was a huge exhibition and both of them were not found again. We gave advertisements in the newspapers. There was no response. And for the next 20 years we have kept looking for them in the same town, every time we go there.

CAPT. BRAIN: How are you going to recognize them now Professor?

PROF. SOUL: By their scarves and dresses. We bought another pair of dresses and scarves and gave an advertisement in the newspapers 20 years back. We still have the dress and the scarves with us.

(Captain Brain slips out of the hall.)

LADY HEART: Professor Mind and Professor Soul what if you meet your lost cousin and niece once again. Will you rethink on your decision?

PROF. MIND: We would jump with joy. For the last 20 years we both have made every attempt to search for them. To find them again would be a big relief and joy for us. We would hug them both and celebrate. Captain Brain returns to the hall with two scarves in his hand.

CAPT. BRAIN: Professor Mind and Professor Soul, do you still recognize these scarves. I think these are the same scarves which your cousin and niece were wearing on the fateful day.

PROF. SOUL: Indeed, where did you find them?

CAPT. BRAIN: Professor Soul, I am your lost cousin.

LADY HEART: And Professor Mind, I am your lost niece.

PROF. SOUL/PROF. MIND: Is it true? How do you know? You were too young to remember then.

LADY HEART: Professor Mind, I and Brain had gone to visit parents and they told us how they had found us roaming around the town, hand in hand, while returning back to their village from a science exhibition. Both our families didn't have children and they regarded us as their own, then onwards. They took us to their village. Later Brain's family shifted to a city and I grew up in the same village.

PROF. SOUL: *(Joyfully)* Dear cousin Brain *(hugs Brain).*

PROF. MIND: Dear niece, how I searched for you. We stayed together for so long and its only now that we know.

(They hug each other and are filled with joy.)

PROF. SOUL: Professor Mind, Captain Brain and Lady Heart, we must be grateful to life for giving us an opportunity to be together and witness a wonderful play of life unfold itself. Professor Mind Congratulations. Congratulations Captain Brain. Congratulations Lady Heart. Let us celebrate and thank life once again.

(Curtains.)

Rest of the play is story of our own lives.

THE SEMINAR

(A play on the importance and purpose of Science)

The characters

PROFESSOR PRAKRATI: Dean of the university. A mature, graceful and understanding personality. Presents the Nature's perspective in the play.

PROFESSOR SELF /SOUL: A scientist at the university. Calm face radiating intelligence and seriousness of purpose . Eyes are filled with a childish inquisitiveness as if trying to learn.

Mr. VIKAS DIMAG: Young, smart and intelligent looking man . Completed his graduation and post graduation from the same university and joined the same university as a scientist. Representing the Brain –the objective .

Miss PRAGATI DILL: A young pretty and charming woman. She too has done her graduation and post graduation from the same university but from different college. Represents the Heart–the subjective.

PROFESSOR MIND: Professor of Philosophy and a playwright at the university. An athletic looking person.

The Story

Since the play is about science and the learning process the story in the play is presented below to simplify and to maintain our focus on science and the process of learning.

Miss Pragati Dill and Mr. Vikas Dimag join the university as young scientists. Professor Self introduces both of them to the Dean of the university - Professor Prakrati.

Professor Prakrati discusses the basics of science with Professor Self, Mr. Vikas Dimag and Miss Pragati Dill. A seminar is organized at the university ,on the basics of science and the learning process . Mr. Vikas and Miss Pragati are given the responsibility of organizing the seminar. A successful seminar is organized at the university. Miss Pragati and Mr. Vikas know and understand more of each other. Miss Pragati and Mr. Vikas who are already associated scientifically with each other as young scientists at the university become related to each other in more than one way.....

Scene of action

The University

The university as described in the play "Tenants". The university is a balanced blend of both the traditional and modern. There is plenty of greenery around - the trees, the gardens, lots of fresh air – Nature at her poetic and pristine beauty. The architecture is exquisite and the town planning excellent. Wide roads, a theatre, an art centre and well equipped labs and classrooms.

Act –1: Professor Self's office in the university. A simple room with a table, a chair for Professor Self and another two for the visitors . Few cabinets with books and office files. Miss Pragati and Mr. Vikas arrive at the office to join as young scientists.

Act –2: Professor Prakrati's office amidst a beautiful garden full of trees with fruits, flowers, and birds .The office is simple, decorated with many landscapes, sceneries and paintings of flowers and trees. A large board close to Professor Prakrati's chair with a poem. A round table with few chairs around.

Act 3: A canteen within the university campus .

Professor Self, Miss Pragati and Mr. Vikas are discussing about life and the importance of various aspects of science along with their research topics and research papers.

Act 4: At Professor Prakrati's office. Professor Self has come to discuss about the seminar. Miss Pragati and Mr. Vikas join the discussion on organizing the seminar.

Act 5: At the seminar Professor Prakrati and Professor Self discuss the success of the seminar with Miss Pragati and Mr. Vikas. Professor Mind joins the discussion .

Act –1

The university has an atmosphere which smells of freshness and purity, scholars with an aptitude for knowledge and acquiring new skills, teachers full of ideas and inspiration and a life full of new and enriching experiences.

Professor Self's office at the university. The office is a simple room with a table, few chairs arranged in the centre of the room, few cabinets with books and office files. Professor Self at work. Few files on his table when the door bell rings. Mr. Vikas and Miss Pragati at the door in the early hours of Monday.

PROF. SELF: Please come in.

(Mr. Vikas and Miss Pragati enter the room.)

Miss Pragati is wearing light green coloured clothes as if to make herself compatible with surrounding nature of the university. Mr. Vikas is wearing a light red coloured shirt which matches the architecture of the university. Both carry with them a small bag, a folder and few pens.

Mr. VIKAS and Miss PRAGATI: Good Morning Professor.

Mr. VIKAS: We both have come to report to you on

our appointment as young scientists at the university. We were told at the office that you have been already sent an intimation regarding our appointment.

PROF. SELF: Good Morning Mr. Vikas and Miss Pragati. Welcome to the university. I received letters regarding your appointment few hours back from the Dean. Please be seated.

(Both take their chairs.)

Mr. VIKAS and Miss PRAGATI: Thank you Professor.

Mr. VIKAS: We have come to report to you with these papers of appointment and our bio-data.

(Both Mr. Vikas and Miss Pragati show their papers of appointment as young scientists at the university. Professor Self accepts the papers, reads them for a while, then.)

PROF. SELF: My heartiest congratulations to both of you on being appointed at the university as young scientists. Its very encouraging and I am very pleased that you have come to work for the same university where you completed your education. Mr. Vikas has completed his post graduation from the same university branch and Miss Pragati has done her post graduation from a different college of same university.Your college records are excellent.

Hope that both of you will bring laurels to the university with your purposeful scientific research.

Mr. VIKAS: Sure Professor.

Miss PRAGATI: Definitely Professor. We both will put our best efforts and stand good to your expectations.

PROF. SELF: Both of you must have been allotted your official residence by now.

Mr. VIKAS: We are staying at the university guest rooms after the appointment.

(Professor Self gives two application forms from his drawer to Vikas and Pragati.)

PROF. SELF: Fill these application forms. I shall forward the letters to the Dean who will provide you with official residence soon .

Mr. VIKAS and Miss PRAGATI: Thank you Professor.

(Both fill the application forms which Professor Self had provided. They return the applications to Professor Self.)

Miss PRAGATI: What about our work Professor? How do we start?

PROF. SELF: You'll have to report to Professor Prakrati the dean of the university with these appointment letters today. For few weeks you shall remain in the apprenticeship of Professor Prakrati .You shall learn about the basics of science and few details about the scientific methods. Professor Prakrati shall first send you on some assignment, for learning the importance of careful observation in science.Then you will be sent to different departments of the university where you will learn about the kind of research the university is involved in and also about proper analysis of scientific data and observations made by you. You will then be assigned different research projects and then enter into the phase of scientific experiments and research. Professor Prakrati shall be your guide during the entire process.

(Professor Self signs the letters of appointment and gives the letters to Mr. Vikas and Miss Pragati.)

PROF. SELF: Take these letters to Professor Prakrati's office and submit to her in person. She will allot you official residence and will give you the entire list of your training schedule.

(Returns the appointment letters to Mr. Vikas and Miss Pragati.)

Miss PRAGATI: Professor you said, we have to report to Professor Prakrati – the Dean of the university. Could you tell us something about her so that we could go to her prepared.

PROF. SELF: Just be yourself - Completely natural. Professor Prakrati will teach you the basics of science and scientific research. She is very methodical about her work and shall take you on scientific journey in a step by step manner. As I said previously, during first few weeks she will teach you about the art and science of proper observation. She will send you on some assignment and ask for a report on the observations, which you made during the assignment. Try to observe orderliness and regularity in the surrounding nature with all inquisitiveness.Then try to raise pertinent questions to her on science. Once you have learnt the art and science of proper observation, she shall test your knowledge and skills of observation and then assign you the departments you will gain experience in. While you work in those departments assigned to you she shall teach you about other aspects of science like generating an appropriate explanation *(hypothesis)* by proper analysis of scientific data and the observations which you made. Subsequently you shall be allowed to work on some scientific projects and learn about devising appropriate experiments to test the hypothesis.

Miss PRAGATI: We are glad that you told us about her. We are quite eager to learn more from her.

PROF. SELF: When you are learning about the art and science of observation, try to ask relevant questions. You can establish your own hypothesis *(explanation)*. Do not try to provide Professor Prakrati with any explanations unless she asks .Only after you have gained experience in various research departments she assigns you, she'll call you again for few weeks and teach you about formulating a plausible explanation *(hypothesis)* about the observations made and the lab data available. The first session will be called descriptive studies – based on observations you made and the second session will be called the analytical – based on the hypothesis you formulate.

The third session shall be called the experimental stage. Only when you have become fully responsible and have known about the importance of the surrounding Nature you shall be allowed to become a full fledged scientist and carry your own scientific research. You will require original ideas and a proper and focused vision to become a successful one.

Mr. VIKAS: Professor you told us that the topics of research shall be assigned by Professor Prakrati. Would our own interest count?

PROF. SELF: Yes. The importance shall be upon your own abilities of proper and careful observations. What you observe shall depend upon your own nature and interest. When you think you have started observing the relevant you shall be assigned the topics according to observations you made. My best wishes to both of you. You have been good students hence be sure of yourself. Rest you'll learn as you progress.

Mr. VIKAS and Miss PRAGATI: Thank you Professor for encouraging us.

Mr. VIKAS: Professor can you just elaborate more upon what you said about observing according to our natures and interest.

PROF. SELF: I shall provide you a scientific explanation to that in terms of present scientific understanding. When you visit Professor Prakrati's office she shall tell you more about observing according to our natures. Coming to the science the observations which you make depend much upon your own location *(space-time location)* and since the location *(space-time)* of observers may differ hence the observations which you make shall be different and according to your own natures.

Miss PRAGATI: Professor how then do we justify science which is and should be based upon the common understanding of the Nature around?

PROF. SELF: Miss Pragati and Mr. Vikas here comes the relevance of the orderliness and regularity in the surrounding nature. In spite of different observations which have been made, Nature by presenting orderliness and regularity in the surroundings shall inspire you to seek exactness in the scheme of life. You shall then learn principles and factors which are simultaneous in spite of differences in our observations. Science then shall become a journey of understanding the regular and orderly principles of Nature and shall inculcate in us the attitude to seek the exactness and truth of life as we progress.

(A thoughtful silence ensues for a while.)

Mr. VIKAS and Miss PRAGATI: Professor we are beginning to understand.

PROF. SELF: I am happy you do. Such shall be essential for our future progress. When you develop good understanding you shall learn to be sincere, honest and truthful about your approach towards life and science.

(A thoughtful silence ensues for a short while.)

PROF. SELF: Make good use of the library and be in sync with the times by going through recent research projects and papers.

Mr. VIKAS: Sure Professor.

Miss PRAGATI: Definitely Professor.

PROF. SELF: Regarding your scientific interest. What exactly inspired both of you to become a scientist?

Mr. VIKAS: Professor first of all our education. I did my graduation from the same college which has instilled in us an aptitude for new knowledge and research. There remains so many questions which I seek answers of. The only way to find solutions I thought was research.

Miss PRAGATI: Education, yes. I would also like to mention the importance of our teachers who have provided us inspiration and guidance. I felt the best way of utilizing our education imparted by our teachers was to put all our skills into research work.

PROF. SELF: Wonderful. You both may have provided different reasons and yet both of you are guided towards the same goals.

Mr. VIKAS: Professor Self, tell us about yourself as well. How you got interested in science?

PROF. SELF: In my case the role of my family is important. My entire family has a tradition of research. I am happy that every member of my family has made some contribution to science. More than inventions and discoveries that everyone contributed to the scheme of life makes me glad and the quest continues till we achieve perfection. The inquisitiveness to find more about the surrounding Nature and know the truth of existence has been the real reason.

Mr. VIKAS: The journey ahead seems inspiring Professor. We eagerly look forward to working with you.

PROF. SELF: In order to work properly with me you will have to report to Professor Prakrati with the appointment letters. Once you have learnt the importance of Nature in life and science, I shall be in a better position to assist and serve our interest and growth.

Mr. VIKAS: Professor why do you say so?

PROF. SELF: Professor Prakrati will teach you the basics of science. Our progress in science will be in coherence with the surrounding Nature. Learning about Nature shall also allow any individual and both of you to act according to his and her best potential.

(A thoughtful silence ensues for a while.)

PROF. SELF: Let me explain, to both of you, in a bit detail. Science relies on a belief that exactness exists in all that occurs. The belief that the exactness exists implies that science is simultaneous to existence. Exactness is about the accuracy and precision of scientific principles. Exactness has broader implications and is akin to making an discovery and invention in science which could be applied to the present. Till we gain complete understanding of the scientific principles the process of deciphering science remains a reflective one i.e. subsequent to proper analysis and experimentation of the data available from the observations made from the creation. In simple terms understanding science is possible only because there is a creation and the process of deciphering science is possible only after proper analysis and experimentation of the observations made from the creation.

Hence as long as the understanding of science reaches exactness science shall pertain to – the existence, the creation and has to be regarded as a reflective study of the observations made from the creation.

Let me for simplicity sake call the creation and existence as 'Nature'. Since Professor

Prakrati shall teach you about the basics of Nature and science involved, you'll have to report to Professor Prakrati to know more about Nature .

Miss PRAGATI: Professor you told that science relies on a belief that exactness exists. Does that imply that science begins with our beliefs?

PROF. SELF: Miss Pragati, in a way yes. You can say so. Science begins with an inquisitiveness to know. Science is about understanding the exactness, so science has to begin with a belief that exactness exists.

Mr. VIKAS: Professor can we also say that science is based on a reason that science is about the very Nature that surrounds us and therefore we have to begin the search of exactness from the very Nature.

PROF. SELF: I will have to agree with you as well . I seem to have discovered an important aspect regarding your natures. Miss Pragati seems to be a attempting to rely on beliefs and Mr. Vikas seems to rely more on reasons. The purpose seems to be same – to decipher the science, to search for exactness and to reach the truth.

Mr. VIKAS and Miss PRAGATI: We agree Professor.

PROF. SELF: Both of you agreed to what was said, simultaneously.

Miss PRAGATI: Professor you mentioned the word simultaneous previously also, while saying that science and existence have to be believed to be simultaneous, to begin our journey of science. We did agree about a common purpose of science, simultaneously. Professor can you elaborate more upon the simultaneous principles of nature.

Mr. VIKAS: Professor, we did agree about the purpose of science simultaneously. We should take into account the fact that different observers may in fact not agree upon the observations made depending upon their location *(space-time)* and relative motion even when occurring simultaneously.

PROF. SELF: Vikas what you mentioned is about simultaneity in science. I have also agreed to the fact that our individual natures are different and observations may be different according to our space-time location and relative movements to each other. According to simultaneity concept in science simultaneously occurring events may be measured differently depending upon relative motion and space time location. Such is necessary to ensure that each individual becomes unique in their observations. Science already regards simultaneity in observations as a relative concept. We shall at present talk about simultaneous principles in Nature and not simultaneity. I said perviously also that science and existence have to be believed as simultaneous to begin our journey of scientific understandings. Just like philosophy in which concepts and percepts have to be together to become logically accurate, similarly in science theoretical and practical aspects have to be together to become scientifically relevant. Hence I shall elaborate upon simultaneous principles along with the practicals at their appropriate time. That Both of you are of separate natures and were studying at different university branches and have come to become scientist at the same place and agreed upon a common purpose of science simultaneouly. This would be sufficient enough to continue our disscussions on science. Concentrate on simpler and basic aspects of science and life till you grasp the details of the factors which are simultaneous. We shall discuss simultaneous principles, and many other scientific concepts at their appropriate forum. Presently we should focus on the basics first. Such would be necessary for proper understanding and also for the future progress because our progress shall depend upon the foundations upon which we stand. We shall proceed in a step by step manner to fulfill the purpose of science which we have agreed upon.

Miss PRAGATI: You also mentioned that our

individual natures are different and unique. Do the differences of our observations make such happen? And Professor does that also imply that individual natures are separate and Nature by presenting orderliness and regularity prepares us to seek the factors which are common in us and conceptually simultaneous in Nature.

Mr. VIKAS: And Professor does such uniqueness make us all a scientist?

PROF. SELF:*(Smiles)* Indeed. At least such uniqueness has made scientist of my entire family. *(Everyone smiles)* That all of us may observe differently and Nature by presenting orderliness and regularity inspires us to seek factors which are common in us and simultaneous in Nature making us all a scientist. The uniqueness of our individual natures does make all members of my family a scientist.

(A thoughtful silence ensues for a short while.)

PROF. SELF: As I said previously as well, keep yourself in sync with the times and with the recent research papers . Learn the basics first and then only you would make a steady progress. The library is a good place to remain abreast with the recent research papers and journals. At the same time try to maintain the uniqueness of your own natures by trying to grasp the ideas and vision, inherent in our everyday experiences.

Try not to miss the experiences of life while becoming a scientist because those very experiences shall inspire you to become successful scientist and carry purposeful research in the future.

Mr. VIKAS and Miss PRAGATI: Certainly Professor.

PROF. SELF: Your curriculum vitae shows that both of you are interested in many co-curricular activities including the theatre. Mr. Vikas must be knowing that the university has an art centre with a theatre. Miss Pragati can also visit the theatre whenever she wishes to. I shall provide you the passes if you wish to attend any art exhibitions or watch any play. There are other attractions too including many tourist spots nearby. You must visit them all. Such shall give life more meaning and purpose.

Mr. VIKAS: Professor I have already shown the theatre to Pragati and showed her some plays. She even visited the art exhibitions and was happy to see the creative talent of the university students. We shall visit the tourist spots near the university soon. And something more important, we are thinking of presenting a play on basics of science in very near future.

PROF. SELF: Good that both you have shown such keen interest in the creative aspects of life. Such is essential to keep us open minded and observant of the creativity in the Nature.

Good that you are writing a play on basics of science. Such shall keep the little artist flourishing along with the scientist in us, while we travel the scientific journey. My best wishes to both of you for the play which you are writing and of course for the scientific journey you have embarked upon. As you learn more of science you shall find yourself in a better position to write a purposeful and meaningful play.

Mr. VIKAS and Miss PRAGATI: Certainly Professor.

Miss PRAGATI: Professor our entire discussion on science has been very fruitful. We have also got some hints towards the kind of play we shall prepare and present. As we progress, writing the play on basics of science shall become much easier.

Mr. VIKAS: Indeed Professor. The play shall also establish the foundations upon which our future scientific progress shall proceed, because the play as you said, shall be upon the basics first. Rest of the science as you said shall be discussed at the appropriate forum.

PROF. SELF: The play on basics of science shall be interesting. Try to utilize an aspect of science which is common to all of us in order to make the play more interesting.

Mr. VIKAS: It shall be a simple play Professor, presenting the basics of science. Only a few necessary technical aspects shall be included. The play shall attempt to present simplified version of science. Importantly we both shall benefit from the play by allowing our understanding to develop a scientific outlook and prepare ourselves for more important scientific research ahead. We shall certainly try to utilize an aspect of science which is common to all of us.

PROF. SELF: I already notice that our concepts regarding science are becoming clearer with proper understanding. Still there is plenty to learn . Professor Prakrati shall make the process of understanding and deciphering science much finer and in fact easier.

Miss PRAGATI: Professor we shall continue to discuss more of science as we progress .

PROF. SELF: Certainly. My best wishes to both of you for your future endeavours.

Mr. VIKAS and Miss PRAGATI: Thank you Professor for encouraging us.

PROF. SELF: We must be grateful to life for allowing us to be together and associate with each other as scientist in our endeavor to decipher science.

(*A thoughtful silence ensues for a while.)*

PROF. SELF: We shall discuss more about science after you have met Professor Prakrati at her office and submitted your appointment letters. She shall definitely assign you some important scientific assignment, initially on observation. We shall discuss more on science of proper observation when we assemble again. Bring your research papers along for a proper discussion.

Mr. VIKAS and Miss PRAGATI: Certainly Professor.

(Mr. Vikas and Miss Pragati collect their appointment letters and get up to leave.)

Mr. VIKAS: Professor, I think we must leave for reporting to Professor Prakrati.

PROF. SELF: Of course. When you complete your play on science invite Professor Prakrati as well. She takes a lot of interest in such activities at the university.

Miss PRAGATI: Thank you Professor for the suggestion.

Mr. VIKAS and Miss PRAGATI: Good Bye Professor.

PROF. SELF: Good bye Miss Pragati and Mr. Vikas. Best wishes to both of you on your scientific journey. Don't forget to bring along your research papers when we meet again.

Mr. VIKAS and Miss PRAGATI: Certainly Professor.

(Mr. Vikas and Miss Pragati leave the office.)

Act –2

Professor Prakrati's office amidst a beautiful garden. Its spring time with flowers blooming all around. The air is rich with the fragrance of the blooming flowers, Nature at her poetic and pristine beauty. Professor Prakrati in a colourful dress which is in sync with the surrounding garden, looks graceful, beautiful and mature. Understands how nature works and sagacious enough to work in coherence with the nature – representative of Nature.

A board above Professor Prakrati's chair. Usually the board is filled with either a thought or with a poem everyday. On the day when Mr. Vikas and Miss Pragati come to her room for submitting their appointment letters, a poem is inscribed on the board. The poem reads....

Nature

Come oh! Child
Look Nature has arranged
The gardens, the playfields
For you to learn

The lessons of life.

When you have learnt well
And have grown into an adult
You shall be guided
To acquire knowledge and skills
So that you could surmount any mountain
Transverse any valley
Travel in the skies as well as the seas
And accept any challenge of life.

When you have learnt, grown
And have become wise
You shall be guided
To reach the truth
From where you could grasp
The essence of life.

(Professor Prakrati is observing flowers in the garden and the surroundings from a window when the door bell rings.)

PROF. PRAKRATI: *(turns towards the door)* Come in .

(Mr. Vikas and Miss Pragati enter inside .)

Mr. VIKAS and Miss PRAGATI: Good morning Professor.

PROF. PRAKRATI: Good Morning to both of you Mr. Vikas and Miss Pragati. Take your seats.

Professor Self called me up and told me about both of you.

Mr. VIKAS: He has given us these appointment letters to be submitted to you.

PROF. PRAKRATI: Keep the letters on the table.

(Professor Prakrati returns to her chair.)

PROF. PRAKRATI: I was just watching the garden outside. I noticed you both coming from Professor Self's office. I saw both of you walking through the pathway. The window is visible through the pathway. Did you notice me looking at both of you?

Miss PRAGATI: Professor, I just had a glimpse of you while entering the garden. I was looking at the beautiful garden around – the flowers, the trees, the flying birds and their nests.

Mr. VIKAS: I too had a glimpse of you while entering the office. I was admiring the architecture of the university buildings and your office which is quite exquisite.

PROF. PRAKRATI: Good you both noticed what you are actually good at, according to your individual natures. Tell me about your backgrounds in the context of how you got influenced to become a scientist.

Miss PRAGATI: Professor I have learnt my early lessons in science from the Nature. The free and open fields, the fresh air, the beautiful landscapes and the natural gardens have been the primary influence upon me which have inspired me to learn more about the surrounding Nature and the science involved. I feel that most of the discoveries we have made is by observing the Nature around therefore I noticed those very aspects while walking through the pathway.

Mr. VIKAS: Professor I have been influenced much by the technological advancement we have achieved. The modern architecture, the inventions and other achievements in the recent times have aroused and are responsible for my interest in science.

PROF. PRAKRATI: Good you both have got influenced and are in sync with your natures.

Mr. VIKAS: Professor could you shed some light upon what you said about observing according to our natures and being in sync with our natures.

PROF. PRAKRATI: I shall give you an example. Did you notice the pathway that led you here to the office?

Miss PRAGATI: Professor I noticed the pathway in just the beginning. The pathway had all the turns and the twist to start with. Once I was in the garden I became busy looking at the poetic and pristine beauty of the surrounding Nature.

Mr. VIKAS: Professor, I noticed the pathway only in the end when I was close to the office and the steps which led us to your office. Before as I said I was looking at the architecture of the office building.

PROF. PRAKRATI: Did you notice that while you were travelling through the pathway in the middle of the garden there was a small flower plant in between the pathway because of which you travelled from two different sides of the pathway?

Mr. VIKAS and Miss PRAGATI: Yes indeed. We both noticed the flower plant because we had to travel from the two sides of the pathway.

PROF. PRAKRATI: Good enough. Do you understand then that what you observe in the surroundings depends much upon your own nature and you both saw the flower plant which was in the middle of the pathway. We seem to agree with each other at places where there is a common understanding, perceptions and aspirations. You have to understand the fact that everyone of us which includes all living organisms are in many ways – inquisitive about the surrounding Nature, trying to decipher the secrets of Nature and trying to evolve. Yes the discoveries and inventions are important. The more important fact is that everyone tries in one way or the other to improve and contribute to the scheme of life and science, makes me glad that perfection is indeed sought after in every earnest. The observations may differ due to the individual natures. Our attempts should be directed towards arriving at ideas where we come to realize the common aspirations, goals and understanding and such is possible when we observe orderliness and regularity in the events of the Nature.

(A thoughtful silence ensues for a while.)

PROF. PRAKRATI: The pathway through the garden also has a story to tell. You entered the garden with interest and inquisitiveness to know and learn more of Nature and science. Miss Pragati said there were turns and many twists to start with. The pathway after the flower plant was straight and as Mr. Vikas said there were few steps before entering the office. The story of science is similar. The beginning is with the inquisitiveness to know about the surroundings filled with all the turns and twists till we acquire a common understanding, then the path becomes straightforward and then the steps of evolution.

Mr. VIKAS: Professor, Do you wish to say that to begin with we do not know and gradually as we travel through the pathway we come to understand the common aspirations and goals and then we begin to evolve.

PROF. PRAKRATI: Yes.

Miss PRAGATI: Professor does the pathway also tell the story, as written in the poem on the board. The poem is simple and I feel the message conveyed to us is about the importance of Nature.

(Miss Pragati rhymes the poem.)

Nature

Come oh! Child
Look Nature has arranged
The gardens, the playfields
For you to learn
The lessons of life.

When you have learnt well
And have grown into an adult
You shall be guided
To acquire knowledge and skills
So that you could surmount any mountain
Transverse any valley
Travel in the skies as well as the seas
And accept any challenge of life.

When you have learnt, grown
And have become wise
you shall be guided
To reach the truth
From where you could grasp
The essence of life.

—

PROF. PRAKRATI: Indeed. I agree with you as well. The simple poem on board and the pathway tell us about the process of evolution and growth. Our awareness passes through different stages. First through the basics, then gradually to more mature levels. Only when we have known the entirety that life gives us a chance to evolve and as the poem says grasp the essence of life.

Mr. VIKAS and Miss PRAGATI: Well said Professor.

PROF. PRAKRATI: Let us now proceed to some official works. As I said you'll have to pass through different stages one by one. First you'll learn about the art and science of proper observation, then arriving at a proper hypothesis *(scientific explanation of observations)* through proper analysis and then the phase of experiments to discover scientific facts. Once you begin discovering the scientific facts, you shall be in a position to apply and invent. You shall understand the importance of each stage only on becoming a complete scientist. You'll have to excel in each stage to become a good scientist. Remember one aspect which is most important. Even though I said that we pass through different stages of growth and evolution, I also say that on reaching the entirety the process becomes simultaneous. For example as full fledged scientist you'll have to observe, analyse, device experiments, discover, invent and apply, get feedback and repeat the entire process again if necessary. Also know that the entire process shall be in coherence to the surrounding Nature and your success with Nature and science shall depend on the originality and comprehensiveness of your ideas.

Miss PRAGATI: We have understood the process you mentioned Professor. Professor Self did give us some details previously and we are prepared to learn our lessons.

Mr. VIKAS: We are ready to pass through the process which you mentioned Professor and ready for any assignment which you assign to us and know more about science.

PROF. PRAKRATI: The assignment which I assign to you shall be based on your own interest and requirements for growth as an individual. As you grow and evolve as individuals and as the citizens of life you shall learn about your own responsibilities and then you shall on your own choose what is important to the scheme of life.

(A thoughtful silence ensues for a while.)

PROF. PRAKRATI: First the basics. To begin with, You'll have to learn the art and science of proper observation. Try to observe regularity and purpose in the scheme of Nature and life. Only when you have learnt making relevant observations you shall enter the next stage.

Miss PRAGATI: Professor we are ready to accept

the responsibilities which are assigned to us.

PROF. PRAKRATI: You both have just completed your education from the same university and are fresh with knowledge and new skills.

Miss PRAGATI: Professor we shall and are still learning and continue to remain learners throughout our life.

Mr. VIKAS: Yes Professor, we both are still students and have to learn a lot before becoming a scientist.

PROF. PRAKRATI: Ok, your first assignment shall be to learn about the very learning process. You will have to visit the university nursery, the schools and the colleges and prepare a detailed report about the learning process- as to how we learn, gain knowledge and acquire skills.

Mr. VIKAS: Professor how will visiting the nursery, the school and the college be useful from the perspective of the learning process?

PROF. PRAKRATI: The best way of learning about the process of learning is to go to the places of learning and watch and participate in the process through which you have evolved yourself. Even though the nursery, the school and the colleges represents only a part of learning, are still important if you consider these places as a part of the gardens and the playfields mentioned in the poem written on the board. Remember your own childhood and the process through which you learnt the lessons of life and became successful enough to become a scientist today.

Your own experiences in life are going to inspire you to make relevant observations, and conduct purposeful research later on. Remember your purpose of becoming a scientist is to discover and invent, for which you'll have to take inspiration from the very life which has given you an opportunity to become a scientist.

Miss PRAGATI: We understand you Professor. The beginning of a scientific journey already looks very inspiring Professor. The method of deciphering science of learning process through visiting the places of learning looks very relevant and interesting .

Mr. VIKAS: Professor Self told us that the purpose of science is to reach exactness.

PROF. PRAKRATI: We shall at present begin the journey of science and concentrate upon the purpose of deciphering the learning process. We shall understand the exactness and essence of life as we pass through the stages of existence.

(A thoughtful silence ensues for a while.)

PROF. PRAKRATI: Take these ID cards for the university staff and you shall be allowed to visit the places of learning.

(Gives Mr. Vikas and Miss Pragati two ID cards from her drawer on the table.)

Mr. VIKAS and Miss PRAGATI: Thank you Professor.

PROF. PRAKRATI: Professor Self has mentioned about providing official residence to both of you.

I am allotting to both of you a residence near the nursery school. The residence is more like a hostel. The school, the college is also nearby. Take these letters of allotment and submit at the university office.

(Signs the letters of allotment and keeps the letters in front of Pragati and Vikas.)

Mr. VIKAS and Miss PRAGATI: Thank you Professor.

(Both take their letters.)

PROF. PRAKRATI: You can take the keys of your hostel rooms from the university office.

Mr. VIKAS and Miss PRAGATI: Ok Professor.

Miss PRAGATI: Professor we are preparing a play on the importance of science. Professor Self told us that you too are interested in the activities of the theatre. Whatever we have discussed today has given us a lot of inspiration regarding science. We shall be able to present the play along with the report on the learning process together. We request you to be the chief guest when we present the play.

PROF. PRAKRATI: Good to hear that both of you have retained your interest in art as well. I am definitely interested in all the creative activities at the university. I shall be present for the play whenever you complete the play and a scientific report on the learning process.

Mr. VIKAS and Miss PRAGATI: Thank you, Professor.

PROF. PRAKRATI: Art has the ability to give satisfaction and happiness with ones own work and science has the capability to inculcate in us the aptitude to search for the truth.

Miss PRAGATI: Professor how does art have the capability to give satisfaction and happiness with ones own work?

PROF. PRAKRATI: Art is inspired out of enriching experiences of life and hence has the capability to impart happiness and satisfaction of having lived and experienced those moments of life.

Miss PRAGATI: Professor you told us that science has the capacity to prepare and inculcate in us the aptitude to search for the truth. Hitherto I felt that science was more about fulfilling the basic requirements of the civilization.

Mr. VIKAS: And I thought that science was about ensuring continuous development of civilization.

PROF. PRAKRATI: The fundamental fact is that science is borne out an inquisitiveness to know more about the surrounding Nature. This inquisitiveness then gradually inspires to seek the exactness and the truth of existence. During the process science fulfils both of what you mentioned.

Mr. VIKAS and Miss PRAGATI: Well said Professor.

Miss PRAGATI: Professor you just mentioned that science is borne out of inquisitiveness to know more about the surrounding Nature. Does that imply that evolution of science depends upon how much related we are with the Nature?

Mr. VIKAS: And Professor what about the role of evolution at the thought level, about associating with ideas in evolution of science?

PROF. PRAKRATI: The essence of learning about science is to be in association with both Nature and ideas. To associate and relate with the minutest details of life including the Nature and Ideas. Evolution at the thought level should also translate into evolution at creative level and unless we evolve at the creative level we cannot know whether we have evolved at the thought level and vice versa.

Miss PRAGATI: Professor Self told us that Nature prepares each individual to act according to his and her best potential.

PROF. PRAKRATI: Nature prepares each individual to seek the truth and essence of life with sincerity and purpose. During the process the individual learns to act according to his best potential because Nature has the capacity to test our abilities and sustainability.

Mr. VIKAS: Professor we shall seek truth with all sincerity and purpose.

Miss PRAGATI: And remain observant of each and every detail of the Nature.

PROF. PRAKRATI: Try to observe Nature in totality and try to look for regularity and purpose in the scheme of Nature. Prepare a detailed scientific report on the learning process in 9 weeks. I shall organize a seminar on the learning process after you have prepared a detailed report on the learning process. Both of you shall be allowed to present a paper on learning process.

Mr. VIKAS: Professor I was wondering as to why you are sending us to the nursery, the school and the colleges. Now I understand the purpose and design.

Miss PRAGATI: Professor, I too understand that you wish us to understand the basics first then through other stages to the present level of understanding. Only then we shall be able to learn, discover, invent and finally seek exactness and truth.

PROF. PRAKRATI: Indeed, my best wishes. Take your appointment letters and hostel allotment letters.

Mr. VIKAS and Miss PRAGATI: Thank you Professor.

(Both collect their letters of appointment and hostel allotment letters.)

PROF. PRAKRATI: Keep visiting the office. We shall

discuss more about Nature and science.

Mr. VIKAS and Miss PRAGATI: Definitely Professor.

Miss PRAGATI: We had a very inspiring discussion today .

Mr. VIKAS: Inspiring and full of responsibilities.

Both get up to leave.

PROF. PRAKRATI: There's an easy way. When you visit the nursery become a child yourself, when in school learn along with others and when in the colleges grow and prepare for the future challenges.

Mr. VIKAS and Miss PRAGATI: Thank you Professor.

(Both leave the room.)

Act –3

A beautiful garden near Professor Self's office. A college canteen near the garden. Early hours of morning, fresh air and rising sun on the horizon. Miss Pragati and Mr. Vikas are seated in chairs around a round table and are taking their morning breakfast. Miss Pragati and Mr. Vikas have started visiting the nursery these days . They carry with them research papers and few journals on science of learning process which are kept on the table. Professor Self comes to the garden.

PROF SELF: Good morning to both of you.

(Professor Self takes and sits on an empty chair.)

Mr. VIKAS and Miss PRAGATI: Good Morning Professor.

Miss PRAGATI: Please share our breakfast Professor and tell us if you wish to order anything else.

PROF. SELF: I just had a light breakfast in the morning. I saw you both from my window and wanted to talk to both of you about the assignment which Professor Prakrati has given to you.

Mr. VIKAS: Professor Prakrati has asked us to prepare a report on the learning process.

Miss PRAGATI: She has asked us to visit the nursery, the school and then the colleges to prepare a scientific report on learning process.

PROF SELF: So both of you are visiting the nursery these days.

Miss PRAGATI: Yes Professor. Professor Prakrati wishes us to understand the basics first then through other stages to the present level of understanding. Only then we shall be able to discover, invent and finally learn and seek exactness and truth.

Mr. VIKAS: Professor I noticed an important fact. Professor Prakrati may have sent us to the nursery the school and the colleges and to the places where we learn. I think her real aim was to teach us the importance of Nature in the learning process .

PROF SELF: Wonderful. I think and feel that both of you have reached the phase of understanding where you are beginning to grasp the purpose of nature and the existence . My congratulations.

Mr. VIKAS and Miss PRAGATI:Thank you Professor.

Miss PRAGATI: In fact we found it very interesting to interact with the kids in a free and undisturbed atmosphere and know more about ourselves and our childhood. The kids asked us so many questions.

PROF SELF: What you actually got to learn and understand is the inquisitiveness among the nursery kids. Young kids are always eager to learn. They are very inquisitive and want to know about each and anything they see. Professor Prakrati's intention is to inculcate in us the same interest of learning which you must have noticed in the kids.

Mr. VIKAS: Your mentioning the inquisitiveness aspect shall be helpful to us throughout our scientific career and also in preparing a scientific report on learning process.

Miss PRAGATI: We got so involved that we played and laughed with the kids. To participate with the kids in their games was a very enriching experience.

PROF SELF: Good that you have found the entire process an enriching one.

Mr. VIKAS: Professor, I think theoretically we can call this process of learning by kids as learning by observation?

PROF SELF: Theoretically, yes. When we include the practical aspect, I think and feel that the process should be called learning by observation and participation. One can admire something and anything from a distance and definitely learn the basic concepts involved and get motivated. The actual learning comes not only by observing but also by participating in the events. You must have known that the sports which you learnt during your nursery must be those which you observed and participated in, on your own. The actual learning comes when we are in the field knowing and experiencing the events on our own. The entire purpose of sending both of you to the nursery school was to teach both of you the importance of practicals along with the theory.

(A thoughtful silence ensues for a while.)

Miss PRAGATI: Professor we got so inspired by the young kids that we have written a poem together. I shall read and rhyme the poem.

(Takes a small note book from her bag and reads a poem written on the first page.)

Miss PRAGATI: Professor the title of the poem is "Little Children rejoice".

(Miss Pragati and Mr. Vikas recite the poem together.)

Little Children Rejoice

Little children rejoice
In bright day light,
The birds sing along the songs of delight.
Dancing and running around
In a merry go round,
Making so much of sound
Some preparing dolls of clay
Everyone busy with their play,
Without any fears to allay.
Innocent and beautiful
In clothes colourful and moods playful,

Making the atmosphere gleeful.
Looking so cute
Their playful shouts,
Can be felt like the music of flute.

PROF. SELF: Well written poetry Miss Pragati and Mr. Vikas. You have described the playful moods of children in most sublime form. My Congratulations to both of you on coming together to write a sublime poem. I shall request Professor Prakrati to include the poem in her office room board.

Mr. VIKAS and Miss PRAGATI: Thank you Professor.

PROF SELF: You should prepare yourself for more responsibilities in near future.

Mr. VIKAS and Miss PRAGATI: Professor we shall be ready for any responsibility.

PROF SELF: Professor Prakrati has called me at her office to discuss about a seminar on science of learning process.

Mr. VIKAS: Professor Prakrati did mention organizing a seminar on the learning process in our previous meeting.

PROF SELF: I expect that she shall grant both of you the responsibility to organize the seminar because both of you are preparing a scientific report on the learning process.

PROF SELF: Next week a seminar shall be organized at another university branch. You both must have attended many seminars before. When you get the responsibility of organizing the seminar at the university, you can accompany me to a seminar at another university branch. I shall take you to the organizers so that you could learn more about organizing a seminar.

Miss PRAGATI: Definitely Professor.

Mr. VIKAS: We would complete our report on learning process before the seminar. We would be free for a week before we join the research faculty according to the list of programmes issued to us hence we shall be able to put every effort necessary in organizing a successful seminar.

PROF. SELF: Take the registration letters for the seminar next week and fill all the relevant details.

(Gives two registration forms to Mr. Vikas and Miss. Pragati.Both read and fill the forms and return the forms to Professor Self.)

PROF. SELF: I'll ensure that both of you get registered for the seminar at other university branch. First I shall confirm with Professor Prakrati that you both have been selected for representing the university at the seminar. Meanwhile, how is your preparation for the play on science and learning proceeding.

Miss PRAGATI: Before you arrived at the canteen we were busy discussing the play on science. We have included a discussion on the science of learning process in the play because learning is common to all. We would be able to discuss science more effectively by doing so. Today morning has also been very interesting. I feel we can include the discussion today, in our play.

Mr. VIKAS: Yes Indeed. Pragati has given a very good suggestion. We both were thinking about the play since few weeks and have acquired definitive thoughts which are supposed to be presented on stage to remain purposeful.

Miss. PRAGATI: We also felt the importance of few lessons the play would present to remain meaningful.

PROF. SELF: Your experiences and the knowledge gained at the nursery must have given you ideas to remain both purposeful and meaningful.

Mr. VIKAS and Miss PRAGATI: Yes Indeed.

PROF. SELF: The journals kept on the table suggest that you are making good use of the library. Can I look at the research papers which you have brought along?

Mr. VIKAS and Miss PRAGATI: Indeed Professor.

(Miss Pragati gives the file containing the research papers to Professor Self. Professor Self takes and reads the research papers for a while.)

Mr. VIKAS: Professor we have included all the details of knowledge available on science of learning process in the files and the research topics so that we could be clear about the aspects which we would observe.

Miss PRAGATI: Professor we have also included the details of the experiments done on the learning process. We have also included the aspects which we have learnt during our visit to the nursery.

PROF. SELF: Good. Both of you are making good progress and would be able to complete your first assignment in correct time.

Mr. VIKAS: Professor our observations at the nursery have given us a clear picture of the learning process. We read a lot of books on learning process and knew the theory part and we still thought there were many unanswered questions as before.

Miss PRAGATI: Professor, I also read a lot about the practical aspects and felt there was much more to learn. The visits to the nursery have opened our minds and we are beginning to understand the learning process in a much better way.

PROF. SELF: As I said earlier keep the practicals and the theory together to acquire a realistic understanding of the learning process. Also remember that the science and existence are simultaneous and only the process of deciphering science, due to the involvement of analysis and experiments is a reflective one.

Mr. VIKAS and Miss PRAGATI: We both shall remember what you said Professor.

PROF. SELF: Ok I shall take leave for a short while. Professor Prakrati has called me at her office. I shall return here after the meeting and shall tell you about her decision about the seminar. Meanwhile both of you can finish your breakfast. When I return to the garden we shall discuss the possibilities which teach us new lessons in life, organizing a seminar for instance.

Mr. VIKAS and Miss PRAGATI: Fine Professor.

(Professor Self leaves for Professor Prakrati's office.)

Mr. VIKAS: Pragati I'll get something more from the canteen. After a light breakfast a glass of juice shall be very refreshing.

Miss PRAGATI: Yes a glass of juice shall be very refreshing. I shall come with you.

(Both go together to the canteen and return to their tables with glasses of fresh juice. Both keep their glasses on the table and periodically sip from the glasses while talking.)

Mr. VIKAS: It will take a while for Professor Self to return from Professor Prakrati's office. We shall continue discussing the report on learning process and the play we are preparing, till then. Professor Self asked us to discuss the possibilities which teach us new lessons in life.

Miss PRAGATI: According to Professor Self, theory and practicals are both important.

Mr. VIKAS: Indeed. Lets discuss the theory.

Miss PRAGATI: And the practical aspects along with.

Mr. VIKAS: Let us begin with the possibility that both of us get the responsibility of learning a new lesson in life.

Miss PRAGATI: Organizing a seminar for instance.

Miss PRAGATI: Since we both do not have prior experience of organizing a seminar, we have to consider organizing a seminar as a new lesson.

Mr. VIKAS: The lesson shall give us the capability to organize any scientific event at the university. Let us discuss what we know first.

Miss PRAGATI: And also the previous experiences we have had about attending a seminar.

Mr. VIKAS: Professor Self included both observation and participation in the learning process. Let us examine how both observing and participating are useful in learning a new lesson.

Miss PRAGATI: We have for instance attended many seminars before as students at the university and have a fair understanding as to what is required to organize a successful seminar. The experience of organizing the seminar shall be like a new lesson and can be regarded as participation in the learning process.

Mr. VIKAS: Observation and participation both.

Miss PRAGATI: Yes. So we can start learning the new lesson.

Mr. VIKAS: We should first know what the seminar

is about?

Miss PRAGATI: On the learning process for instance.

Mr. VIKAS: We must also know whatever is already known about the topic of discussion and the research possibilities.

Miss PRAGATI: We can invite experts who have knowledge and are doing research on the process of learning.

Mr. VIKAS: We'll have to accept full responsibility of organizing the seminar. Professor Prakrati has told us that we both shall be allowed to present our papers during the seminar. I am thinking of presenting the theoretical aspects of the learning process including details about all the knowledge about learning process available till date and the possible research areas.

Miss PRAGATI: And I shall present all the practical aspects including the previous experiments on learning process and the research aspects.

Mr. VIKAS: To present papers on knowledge available and the experiments conducted till date shall be quite easy for both of us. Professor Self asked both of us to discuss about learning new lessons. We must now focus on new areas of research.

Miss PRAGATI: The new areas of research can only be discussed in the light of previous knowledge and the experiments already conducted. Hence we must not lose the background upon which we shall base our research. I agree that to present the papers on knowledge and experiments till date shall be easier task. We can refer to many standard books and journals. And I agree that at present our focus should be upon the new areas of research i.e, upon the process of learning new lessons.

(Mr. Vikas takes a small pad and a pen and makes notes while talking.)

Miss PRAGATI: The first possibility is that we learn new lessons by chance, a kind of serendipity when we try to solve the difficulties that arise in the due course of our life.

Mr. VIKAS: Second possibility is that we learn through a systematic trial and error method where we try to resolve and in spite of errors find solutions finally.

Mr. VIKAS: The third possibility is that living organisms have the capability to analyse the previous experiences and devise means to find new solutions.

Miss PRAGATI: We can also take advice and seek solutions from those who have more experience than us and learn new lessons during the process. For instance Professor Prakrati and the organizers of previous seminars at the university. There always exists someone who knows something and teaches us and at least inspires us to learn new lessons in life.

Mr. VIKAS: We can utilize the present methodology of science in deciphering the process of learning a new lesson.

Miss PRAGATI: We must regard ourselves fortunate that we just visited the nursery and have seen the young kids learn. We both can discuss the process of learning new lessons in the light of new experiences at the nursery.

Mr. VIKAS: Indeed, we both have to visit the school and the colleges at the university and shall get opportunity to learn more about the learning process. We must search for new knowledge in the light of new observations we make. We shall continue our discussion on all the possibilities we talked about, as we proceed with our training. I have already prepared a list of the possibilities we discussed today.

(Professor Self is seen returning to the garden from Professor Prakrati's office.)

PROF. SELF: Congratulations, Professor Prakrati has given both of you the responsibility to organize the seminar. She has given the papers about the possible topics of discussion. Both of you shall be allowed to begin the proceedings by presenting a scientific report on the process of learning.

Mr. VIKAS and Miss PRAGATI: Thank you Professor.

Mr. VIKAS: We were just discussing about the same process of learning. The report which we are preparing shall be of immense benefit for us. We can present the same report in the seminar.

PROF. SELF: Yes Indeed. The report on the role of observation and participation in the process of learning. And also the process of learning new lessons in life. I have sent your registration letter for the seminar at the university branch. You can accompany me to the seminar. Meanwhile you can present a gist of what you discussed about learning new lessons.

Mr. VIKAS and Miss PRAGATI: Thank you Professor for getting us registered.

Miss PRAGATI: Professor first we regarded organizing the seminar as a new lesson to keep the theory and the practicals together.

Mr. VIKAS: *(Reads from the pad)* Professor then we discussed some possibilities about learning new lessons. The first possibility is that we learn new lessons by chance, a kind of serendipity when we try to solve the difficulties that arise in the due course of our life.

PROF. SELF: Since we are students of science we shall not leave anything on chance. Let chance make entry if so wishes to. As scientist we shall rely on facts. I do however agree with the possibility that we learn new lessons when we try to solve the difficulties that arise in the due course of our life. The intension to solve and learn is important to begin with.

Miss PRAGATI: Second possibility is that we learn through a systematic trial and error method where we try to resolve and in spite of errors try new methods and find solutions finally.

PROF. SELF: Good. If we combine the first and the second possibilities the method can be called "Sequential attempts to solve and learn".

Mr. VIKAS: The third possibility is that living organisms have the capability to analyse the previous experiences and devise means to find new solutions.

PROF. SELF: The previous experiences are important in the learning process. The importance is upon correctness of the lesson learnt which shall require a proper analysis.

Miss PRAGATI: Another possibility which we discussed is that we can take advice and seek solutions from those who have more experience than us and learn new lessons during the process.

PROF. SELF: Yes the possibility that someone might have tried to learn similar lesson and taking advice from such people is also fine and yet the attempt to seek solutions and learn will have to be ones own since the lesson which we are learning is new.The possibility that we learn new lessons exists only when we are facing the events and situations of life on our own. We all become unique by doing so because all of us face different situations in life, some may be similar but never same.

(A thoughtful silence ensues for a short while.)

Mr. VIKAS: Professor we have decided to consider more possibilities as we proceed through our training.

PROF. SELF: Decent enough. We never know what we might discover. All that is required of us is to remain vigilant of every detail and possibility in life. We can assemble at the same place every Saturday to discuss more on learning process.

Mr. VIKAS: Sure Professor.

Miss PRAGATI: Definitely Professor.

PROF. SELF: Ok, I shall leave for my office.

Miss PRAGATI: We are also going to the nursery to complete our assignment.

Mr. VIKAS: And complete our report on the learning process.

Miss PRAGATI: Thank you Professor it was nice to talk to you.

PROF. SELF: I am happy that you both have shown the prerequisite interest and inquisitiveness to become a good scientist.

(Professor Self leaves for his office.)

(Mr. Vikas and Miss. Pragati also leave for their assignments.)

ACT- 4

Professor Prakrati's office. Professor Prakrati and Professor Self are discussing about the seminar. Mr. Vikas and Miss Pragati are visiting the colleges of the university and have prepared most of their report. Mr. Vikas and Miss Pragati have recently attended the seminar which Professor Self got them registered to and since then, have taken full responsibility of organizing the seminar.

A new poem is written on the board in Professor Prakrati's room. The poem is same as was written by Miss Pragati and Mr. Vikas during their visit to the nursery schools and reads....

Little Children Rejoice

Little children rejoice
In bright day light
The birds sing along the songs of delight.
Dancing and running around
In a merry go round
Making so much of sound
Some preparing dolls of clay

Everyone busy with their play
Without any fears to allay.
    Innocent and beautiful
    In clothes colourful and moods playful
    Making the atmosphere gleeful.
Looking so cute
Their playful shouts
Can be felt like the music of flute.

(It's the same poem which was written by Pragati and Vikas together.)

PROF. PRAKRATI: Professor Self, How is your preparation of the seminar, going on? I hope Mr. Vikas and Miss. Pragati are helping you out with the seminar.

PROF. SELF: The preparations are on the full swing Professor. We have prepared invitation letters for all the delegates and the speakers with the details about the entire seminar. Mr. Vikas and Miss Pragati have almost completed their project report on the process of learning. Both are visiting the colleges these days. Both shall be the first speakers in the seminar. They are also assisting me in organizing the seminar. All of us went to a science seminar at the university branch few days back. Since then Vikas and Pragati have taken entire responsibility of organizing the seminar.

PROF. PRAKRATI: I would like to read their report once the report on the process of learning is ready. Since both have taken the responsibility of organizing the seminar, we must invite both Vikas and Pragati for our discussion on the seminar.

PROF. SELF: I have already sent a word to both Vikas and Pragati about our discussion on the seminar. Both shall soon be with us.

(The door bell rings.)

PROF. PRAKRATI: Come in.

(Mr. Vikas and Miss Pragati enter the room.)

Mr. VIKAS and Miss PRAGATI: Good Morning Professor Prakrati. Good Morning Professor Self.

PROF. PRAKRATI: Take your seats. We were discussing about the seminar. I am happy to know that you have prepared invitation letters for the delegates and speakers with the entire programme.

(Mr. VIKAS and Miss PRAGATI take their seats.)

Mr. VIKAS and Miss PRAGATI: Thank you Professor. Our experience at the seminar organized at another university branch has helped us a lot. Professor Self has been with us all throughout.

PROF. PRAKRATI: Professor Self told me that you have almost completed your report on the learning process.

Mr. VIKAS: Yes indeed. We are visiting the colleges these days and have spent three weeks at both the nursery and schools and have learnt a lot about the learning process. We are visiting the colleges of the university for a week. We are about to complete our report in another two weeks .

(Pragati and Vikas notice the poem on the board.)

Miss PRAGATI: Professor, the poem!

PROF. PRAKRATI: Professor Self told me that both of you have written the poem together, hence I included the poem on the board.

Miss PRAGATI: Professor, we have had a great experience learning about the kids and children and have learnt a lot about ourselves through them. To observe young kids and children in free and undisturbed atmosphere was indeed a rewarding experience. We enjoyed and learnt with every moment we spent at the places of learning.

Mr. VIKAS: Professor the experience was like revisiting our childhood days and learning about how we learnt ourselves.

PROF. PRAKRATI: I am happy that both of you found the entire process rewarding enough. My congratulations. Your next assignment is the seminar. Keep your report ready by then. I shall read the entire report and shall call you for a discussion on the report before the seminar begins.

Miss. PRAGATI: Professor we are preparing two separate reports on the learning process.

Mr. VIKAS: Professor I am presenting a report on the theoretical aspects, including details of all the knowledge about learning process available till date and the possible research areas.

Miss PRAGATI: And I shall present all the practical aspects, including the previous experiments on learning process and the research aspects.

Prof. PRAKRATI: I expected both of you to do so. Your natures are such that both of you shall appear to be different and separate even though in actuality both of you are supposed to and meant to complement each other during the process of becoming full fledged scientist.

Mr. VIKAS and Miss PRAGATI: We both are also trying to present a combined report including both the theory and the practicals.

PROF. PRAKRATI: In order to present a combined report both of you must understand the importance of complementing each other and the role of science in making you realize so. We shall discuss the importance of association in science. Science starts once we begin to associate with the surrounding Nature only then we observe orderliness and regularity. First try to understand as to why both of you were sent to the nursery, the school and the college together. For doing so read again the poem which you have written.

(Mr. Vikas and Miss Pragati read and rhyme the poem written on the board together.)

PROF. PRAKRATI: The poem shows that both of you were excited about observing young kids in the nursery and thoroughly enjoyed them playing. You both must have remembered your own childhood days. The entire process must have allowed you to prepare a scientific report also. The purpose was to make you understand as to how both the subjective and objective are co-acting together.

PROF. SELF: Being subjects we experience the subjective aspects simultaneously with the experience and the objective aspects in spite of being simultaneous can be known only after a proper analysis and hence slightly later than the subjective aspects. The time difference in understanding is arising due to us being the subjects ourselves. Once subjective and objective are known, new methods can be applied which make the learning process simpler and easier.

Mr. VIKAS: Professor that implies that the subjective and objective aspects are simultaneous and we experience them together. Only because we have to analyse the experiences to know the objective aspects that the differences are arising.

PROF. PRAKRATI: You both can understand in a more simple way. Both of you passed the same phases from nursery to school, then to college and then to the scientist. Both of you must have experienced and played just like the kids in your poem during your childhood. The fact is that only as a scientist you learnt about the learning process even though both of you learnt your lessons and grew simultaneously with those experiences at nursery, the school and the colleges.

Mr. VIKAS and Miss PRAGATI: *(Ecstatically)* Indeed.

Mr. VIKAS: Professor Self told us once that the deciphering science was a reflective process and exactness and simultaneous principles can be understood only on reaching the exactness.

Miss PRAGATI: And does that imply that exactness is indeed possible?

PROF. PRAKRATI: Science includes apart from observation, a proper analysis and experiments to confirm the findings. Even though science was simultaneous with the observations which were made and yet the knowledge comes only after proper analysis and experiments hence process of deciphering science can be called reflective. Science as such is simultaneous with existence provided we have known the science completely. And since I have already said that science is simultaneous hence I also say that understanding exactness is possible. The actual purpose of science as I told you before is to seek the truth of existence.

Mr. VIKAS and Miss PRAGATI: We have begun to understand Professor.

PROF. PRAKRATI: Let us simplify the process. Let both Vikas and Pragati present the reports which they are preparing and let Professor Self present a report which summarizes both the aspects together. Such shall be necessary to include the importance of your individual natures as they are and also give importance to both practical aspects and the theoretical aspects. Soon Pragati and Vikas shall also understand the simultaneous principles and then they shall begin preparing both the reports together without the distinction of the subjective and the objective.

PROF. SELF: Professor we have been discussing the science of learning with each other in the morning hours every Saturday and Sunday. I think and feel that I shall be able to present a report which includes the importance of both the subjective and objective aspects.

PROF. PRAKRATI: We shall discuss a little bit more about simultaneous principles. I shall ask Pragati and Vikas about their opinions about some important aspects about science and the learning process and Professor Self shall attempt to integrate both the aspects. I shall add to the discussion whenever is necessary.

Mr. VIKAS and Miss PRAGATI: Yes Professor.

PROF. SELF: Fine professor.

PROF. PRAKRATI: Lets begin our discussion with

Science. Express your views about the origin of science.

PROF. PRAKRATI: Need is the mother of invention. Science emerges out of attempts to find means to fulfill the necessities.

Mr. VIKAS: Science emerges out of thoughts which guide us to know more about the surrounding Nature.

PROF. SELF: Science is borne out of inquisitiveness to know more about the surrounding nature and during the process fulfills our natural necessities.

PROF. PRAKRATI: Express your views about the Scientific progress. What do you regard as evolution in science?

Mr. VIKAS: I regard scientific evolution as the evolution at the level of thought i.e. about developing new ideas which make the new inventions possible.

Miss PRAGATI: I regard scientific evolution as the progress which improves the living conditions of everyone at the creation level.

PROF. SELF: Consider so that evolution at the thought level should also translate into evolution at the creation level and vice versa. Scientific evolution must involve both evolution at the thought level and the creation level.

PROF. PRAKRATI: While acquiring knowledge, how do we proceed?

Miss PRAGATI: Our knowledge is derived from

experiences, hence we proceed from concrete *(experiences)* to the abstract *(knowledge)*.

Mr. VIKAS: Our knowledge has roots in intuition and hence we proceed from abstract *(thoughts)* to the concrete *(experience)*.

PROF. SELF: Consider that we proceed from known particular instances to the universal principles while acquring knowledge.

PROF. PRAKRATI: That eventually we learn, grow, acquire knowledge and understand life i.e. we proceed in a way which is natural for us - the natural way. The natural way is about being ourselves and regarding the entire life as a learning process.

"We are like little children on earth,
free to learn ,
till we gain enough knowledge,
to reach the wise one."

Such must be the journey of gaining knowledge, the natural way.

PROF. SELF: In the context of the day when we are discussing, science describes matter as wave or particle?

Mr. VIKAS and Miss PRAGATI: Both.

PROF. SELF: Good, now you shall be able to understand the importance of proper association in science and the importance of simultaneous principles. The purpose of organizing seminar was to make you understand the importance of proper association in the learning process and science. We have told previously as well that both of you could complement each other In spite of separate natures. And we expect that both of you shall complement and associate with each other so that a successful seminar on science of learning could be organized.

PROF. PRAKRATI: Coming to the seminar, we have to arrange for proper stay of the delegates. I shall be allotting university guest houses to the delegates. Send me the list of delegates invited for the seminar.

Miss PRAGATI: The college catering staff at the canteen have been given the responsibility to prepare food for the delegates. A menu has been prepared for the seminar.

Mr. VIKAS: We have to prepare mementos for the delegates and the speaker as an encouragement of sorts. It will be like a positive reinforcement for their efforts.

Miss PRAGATI: I have prepared a small list of tasks and would complete every thing in time.

PROF. PRAKRATI: We have had a very fruitful discussion today about the seminar and the learning process. We shall discuss more as we progress. You can call or come to my office anytime if anything is required.

PROF. SELF: Thank you Professor.

Mr. VIKAS and Miss PRAGATI: Thank you Professor.

(Vikas and Pragati leave the office.)

Act –5 (The Seminar)

The Seminar is in full swing at the university. After the inauguration ceremony a small lunch party is held in the university lawn. The lunch was followed by the research paper presentation in the seminar hall. The seminar hall at the university is full of delegates. Mr. Vikas, Miss Pragati and Professor Self and other delegates have finished their presentation. Professor Prakrati is congratulating Miss Pragati and Mr. Vikas for their presentation near the podium.

PROF. PRAKRATI: The seminar has been a resounding success.The presentations were well prepared, full of knowledge and experience. I congratulate Mr. Vikas and Miss Pragati for such decent arrangement and also for their wonderful presentation. The entire discussion was of immense benefit for the understanding of learning process and the Nature.

Mr. VIKAS: Professor you had asked us to associate properly with each other to organize the seminar. I think we must have lived upto the expectations.

PROF. PRAKRATI: Certainly.

Miss PRAGATI: Professor, organizing the seminar was a new lesson for us. We have learnt the importance of proper observation and participation in learning.

Mr. VIKAS: We have also learnt about recent research areas which shall be useful to us throughout our career as scientists.

Miss PRAGATI: The experience at the nursery, the schools and the colleges have renewed our foundations of education and have given us a scientific perspective of looking at the experiences.

PROF. PRAKRATI: I am happy that you both liked the entire exercise. You shall soon join the research section of the university and shall be involved in analysing the scientific data and prepare scientific hypothesis *(explanations)*. It will be like finishing the nursery education and joining the school.

(Everyone smiles.)

(Professor Self arrives near the podium.)

PROF. SELF: Congratulations Mr. Vikas and Miss Pragati on a wonderful presentation and for organizing a successful and knowledgeable seminar.

Mr. VIKAS and Miss PRAGATI: Thank you Professor .

PROF. PRAKRATI: Congratulations to you also Professor. You prepared a good report combining both the aspects which Vikas and

Pragati had presented. Overall a good beginning to the academic year.

Mr. VIKAS and Miss PRAGATI: Our congratulations too Professor .

PROF. SELF:Thank you Professor. Thank you Mr. Vikas and Miss Pragati. The success of the seminar gives me immense happiness. Mr. Vikas and Miss Pragati associated so nicely with each other and have worked in such close collaboration that everything became so easy for us.

Mr. VIKAS and Miss PRAGATI: Thank you Professor.

PROF. SELF: The play which you were preparing must have got a lot of boost and inputs from the seminar.

Miss PRAGATI: The seminar has allowed both of us to learn so many aspects of life together and shall indeed be pivotal in making us learn more about science and the learning process. We have indeed benefited a lot and the play we are preparing shall also get a lot of boost and inputs.

Mr. VIKAS: Professor Mind - Professor of philosophy at the university has been assisting us in writing the play. We invited him to the seminar and he says the play shall be ready soon. He too was happy with the way the seminar was conducted and says that he shall be able to present a better play on learning and science after attending the seminar.

PROF. SELF: Professor Mind is a close associate of

mine and is presently staying with me at my residence. He is a good playwright and since he attended the seminar, so the play shall remain scientifically relevant. He is presenting another play titled "Tenants". I think and feel that both the plays can be presented together to highlight the importance of both art and science.

Mr. VIKAS: Yes he did tell us about the play and we have decided to present both the plays together on the same day. He has given us passes for "Tenants". He says he shall complete writing both the plays together.

PROF. SELF: Professor Mind has the habit of unifying different aspects of life. According to him the solutions of science, art, philosophy, and most importantly life shall be found on unifying them all. So most likely the play he shall prepare will be an effort in such a direction and with such an intension. He is an interesting personality and has his own concepts of living life. We have been staying together ever since he was appointed as the Professor of philosophy at the university.

Mr. VIKAS: Professor Mind has asked us to be prepared to play major roles in the plays and he has asked us to provide all the details about the meetings we have had with both of you.

PROF. SELF: Such would be wonderful. Both of

you must get the opportunity to play the lead roles in a play of science. As I said previously also such would be necessary for presenting the balance of the Nature. Of course a character in the play should also present the role of nature in the evolution of science. I shall provide Professor Mind some details about the meetings we had together while preparing the reports on the learning process. Just like the seminar both of you would complement each other perfectly in the play also.

(Professor Mind arrives near the podium. They share greetings with each other.)

PROF. SELF: Professor Mind we were just talking about the plays which you are preparing on art and science. I shall provide you all the details which you wanted regarding the meetings which we had while preparing reports on the learning process.

Prof.MIND: The seminar has given me valuable inputs about the learning process and I shall be able to write a play on the basics of science along with another play "Tenants" on the importance of art. Both the plays can be presented together to present the relevance of both science and arts. In the play on the basics of science Mr. Vikas Dimag and Miss Pragati Dill shall be playing major roles including few more characters who shall present the logical aspects pertaining to science. I have selected Vikas and Pragati to play the major roles because both have associated so nicely with each other in many ways and also due to the fact they both represent the future of scientific development at the university.

PROF. PRAKRATI: Don't you all think, feel and sense that Vikas and Pragati must have known each other before joining the university because the way both have worked and collaborated with each other is amazing.

PROF. SELF: Yes indeed. I also think and feel and am pretty certain that both of you have some common link which makes them complement each other so nicely. Our parents stayed together as neighbours when we were small kids. Our parents say that we used to play together. Vikas and his family then shifted to a different place. So in a way we are childhood friends. We invited our parents at the seminar. They met each other after so many years at the lunch party.

PROF. PRAKRATI: So both of you knew each other so well from the very beginning.

MR. VIKAS:When we met each other after the selection as scientist at the university, we too didn't recognize each other. Only when we started talking about our parents that we came to know about each other.

MISS PRAGATI: *(Smiles)* And Professor our parents

were also happy to see both of us work and learn together and have suggested us to consider a long term relationship with each other.

Mr. VIKAS: Dear Pragati we are already associated with each other as scientists. We are scientists and can continue to be together and look at everything with a scientific attitude.

Miss PRAGATI: *(Smiles)* Dear Vikas the fact is that we both know and understand each other so nicely that we won't have much difficulty even relating with each other through marriage. And of course we can continue to look at everything around with a scientific attitude even after marriage. We can regard marriage as a scientific association.

(Everyone smiles.)

Prof. PRAKRATI: Professor Self we discussed about science, about learning process, about simultaneous nature of the subjective and the objective aspects in learning process and about role of association in science. Vikas and Pragati have gone a step ahead and are about to marry.

Everyone smiles.)

Prof. SELF: Professor "a child is the father and mother of a man and woman respectively". The association between Vikas and Pragati has been good for science and a relationship shall ensure their overall growth, development, balance and equilibrium in life. Miss Pragati and Mr. Vikas both of you stand for scientific development at the university. Continue with your good efforts. You shall be joining the research section of the university in next few days. My Best wishes to both of you. Keep the little artist and scientist flourishing.

Prof. MIND: And since you are getting associated in other ways also and many of your conditioned responses of learning would become unconditional soon, so the word 'little' should ring more bells.

(Everyone smiles.)

(Refer to the meaning of the terms unconditional and conditional in definitions given after the play)

Miss PRAGATI: Professor you told us that Nature guides us to seek and reach truth. We still haven't understood, how?

Prof. PRAKRATI: Nature makes us aware of an aspect which exists outside our individual existence. The question is what? The truth is about determining the answer to the question and finding that which not only constitutes but also assimilates all other simultaneous factors. *(Remember)* In science what we regard as measurement is actually a comparison.

Miss PRAGATI and Mr. VIKAS: Thank you Professor.

Prof. SELF: I often say at my house, "we must be

grateful to life for giving us an opportunity to be together and learn so much about life and associate with each other as scientists in our endeavour to decipher science and to learn through a wonderful seminar about science, arts and life."

Prof. PRAKRATI: Professor Self let me add a little more "We must be grateful to life for giving us an opportunity to be together, to associate and relate with Nature and search for exactness and truth of life. And let me repeat the seminar is just an example, the extension is to the entire life".

Rest of the play is again the story of our own lives.

Definitions of basic terms used in the play

1) Learning - refers to the changes brought about by experiences. Psychologically learning refers to any permanent behaviour (behaviour potential) brought about by an experience. From philosophical perspective we can regard learning as the process of acquiring new knowledge and skills through experience.

According to the psychologists of the present times the learning is of several basic forms and includes:

A) Classical conditioning: A form of learning in which one stimulus comes to serve as a signal for the occurrence of a second stimulus between them. A stimulus is a physical event capable of effecting behaviour. The stimulus can be unconditional (natural) or conditioned. An unconditional stimulus can evoke an unconditioned response the first time its presented and a conditioned stimulus can be paired by repetition with a unconditioned stimulus to elicit a response.

B) Operant conditioning (Learning based on consequences): A process through which organisms learn to repeat behaviours that yield positive results or permit them to avoid from negative results. For example presenting mementos to the delegates in the play is a type of positive reinforcement for their efforts.

C) Observational learning: The form of learning from observing and later action on new information, behaviours and concepts demonstrated by others.

For details refer to psychology text books.

Scientific Methodology: the play presents a brief look at the scientific methodology. Few terms used in the play include:

A) Observation: To study the events of nature in a free and undisturbed atmosphere. The observer observes and measures but does not intervene.

B) Analysis: A process of establishing relationships between various variables influencing the events of nature.

C) Experiments: An active attempt to change the factors and determinants of an event to test the accuracy of the relation established by analysis between the variables.